To _____

From _____

Often through the passing days
We feel deep down inside
Unspoken thoughts of friendship
And fond, admiring pride.
But words can say so little
When the heart is overflowing,
And often those we love the most
Just have no way of knowing
The many things the heart conceals
And never can impart,
For words seem so inadequate
To express what's in the heart.

THE HELEN STEINER RICE FOUNDATION

Whatever the celebration, whatever the day, whatever the event, whatever the occasion, Helen Steiner Rice possessed the ability to express the appropriate feeling for that particular moment in time.

A happening became happier, a sentiment more sentimental, a memory more memorable because of her deep sensitivity to put into understandable language the emotion being experienced. Her positive attitude, her concern for others, and her love of God are identifiable threads woven into her life, her work . . . and even her death.

Prior to her passing, she established the HELEN STEINER RICE FOUNDATION, a nonprofit corporation whose purpose is to award grants to worthy charitable programs that aid the elderly, the needy, and the poor. In her lifetime, these were the individuals about whom Mrs. Rice was greatly concerned.

Royalties from the sale of this book will add to the financial capabilities of the HELEN STEINER RICE FOUNDATION, thus making possible additional grants to various qualified, worthwhile, and charitable programs. Because of her foresight, her caring, and her deep convictions, Helen Steiner Rice continues to touch a countless number of lives. Thank you for your assistance in helping to keep Helen's dream alive.

Virginia J. Ruehlmann, Administrator
The Helen Steiner Rice Foundation
Suite 2100, Atrium Two
221 East Fourth Street
Cincinnati, Ohio 45202

Helen Steiner Rice

Blossoms of

Friendship

Compiled by Virginia J. Ruehlmann

Fleming H. Revell Company
Tarrytown, New York

Scripture quotation is taken from the Holy Bible, New International Version, copyright © 1973, 1978, 1984 International Bible Society. Used by permission of Zondervan Bible Publishers.

Jacket and interior illustrations by Maureen Ruckdeschel

Library of Congress Cataloging-in-Publication Data
Rice, Helen Steiner.
  Blossoms of friendship / Helen Steiner Rice.
      p.   cm.
  ISBN 0-8007-1664-7
  I. Title.
PS3568.I28B5   1992
811'.54—dc20
                                                    91-41049
                                                    CIP

Copyright © 1992 by Virginia J. Ruehlmann and
The Helen Steiner Rice Foundation
Published by the Fleming H. Revell Company
Tarrytown, New York 10591
Printed in the United States of America

Dedicated to
Friends recently made,
Friends of long standing,
Friends yet to be, and

To that very special friend
Who finds beauty in
Each person and in every flower
Growing in the garden of God
Here on earth!

Contents

From the forest violet to the cultivated orchid
From flower box plantings to cottage gardens
From clustered wildflowers to palatial formal grounds
From arrangements in tiny wicker baskets
    to arrangements in priceless porcelain containers
Flowers possess a language of their own.
The message that they send is one that is understood in
all parts of the world, irrespective of the native tongue:

God loves mankind so much that He
shares beauty and love through
His flowers.

VJR

Introduction

A lifetime without one friend is like a garden without a single flower. Practice the art of gardening. Plant and cultivate the seed of friendship. May it blossom and grow wherever your garden of love is planted.

One of the highest compliments ever spoken of another individual contains the words, "This is my friend." It is impossible to estimate the impact, the meaning, the deep appreciation, and the love conveyed by these words. It is possible to sense the affection, the acceptance, the honest approval implied, as well as the trust, confidence, and mutual respect suggested.

A friend is ready to assist you, to comfort you, to defend you, to encourage you, to forgive you, to listen to you, to share joys and sorrows with you, to sympathize with you, to be happy for you, to congratulate you without a twinge of envy, and to remember only the good and pleasant memories of experiences mutually shared.

To have one such friend in a lifetime is truly a gift; to have more than one, is a treasure beyond compare. So value and honor, guard and hold in high esteem such precious friendships that you share.

The poetry of Helen Steiner Rice affords excellent insight into making, keeping, and sustaining friendships. May you have—and may you be—a very special friend. It is my hope that this book will aid you in accomplishing that goal.

. In friendship's sake,
Virginia J. Ruehlmann

Friendship's Flowers

Life is a garden,
    good friends are the flowers,
And time spent together,
    life's happiest hours;
For friendship, like flowers,
    blooms ever more fair
When carefully tended
    by dear friends who care;
And life's lovely garden
    would be sweeter by far
If all who passed through it
    were as nice as you are.

A real friend is one who overlooks your broken-down gate and admires the flowers in your garden.

Author Unknown

Carnations

Hide, oh hide those hills of snow
Which thy frozen bosom bears,
On whose tops the pinks that grow
Are of those that April wears!
                    John Fletcher

Years and years of care, perseverance, and considerable amounts of dedication have been devoted by many to the development of our present-day Carnation from the small-clove Pink known as *Dianthus caryophyllus*.

Cultivated by the Greeks long before the days of Christ, Pinks became known as "*Dianthus,* the Divine Flower." The name *Dianthus* eventually came to refer to the entire family of Pinks. Because of their scent and beauty, Pinks were used in wreaths and garlands for the head (*Coronae*). From this use in floral coronets, to the English word *coronation,* the transition to the name Carnation for the cultivated variety of Pink was derived.

Clove-scented Pinks were popular for flavoring wines in early Rome and used for medicinal purposes in drinks by the French in the thirteenth century to reduce fever during the plague in Tunis. Because of this association, the Pink was originally called *Tunica.*

In the language of flowers, a double red Pink is a sign of pure and ardent love, and a white Pink suggests ingeniousness and talent.

Heart Gifts

It's not the things that can be bought
   that are life's richest treasure,
It's just the little heart gifts
   that money cannot measure.
A cheerful smile, a friendly word,
   a sympathetic nod
Are priceless little treasures
   from the storehouse of our God.
They are the things that can't be bought
   with silver or with gold,
For thoughtfulness and kindness
   and love are never sold.
They are the priceless things in life
   for which no one can pay,
And the giver finds rich recompense
   in giving them away.

Courtesies of a small and trivial character are the ones which strike deepest in the grateful and appreciating heart.

Henry Clay

Fulfillment

Apple blossoms bursting wide
  now beautify the tree
And make a springtime picture
  that is beautiful to see.
Oh, fragrant lovely blossoms,
  you'll make a bright bouquet
If I but break your branches
  from the apple tree today.
But if I break your branches
  and make your beauty mine,
You'll bear no fruit in season
  when severed from the vine.
For as the flowering branches
  depend upon the tree
To nourish and fulfill them
  till they reach futurity,
We, too, must be dependent
  on our Father up above,
For we are but the branches
  and He's the tree of love.

Behind every flower stands God.
Japanese Proverb

Everybody Everywhere Needs
Somebody Sometime

Everybody, everywhere,
  no matter what his station,
Has moments of deep loneliness
  and quiet desperation.
For this lost and lonely feeling
  is inherent in mankind
It is just the Spirit speaking
  as God tries again to find
An opening in the worldly wall
  man builds against God's touch,
For he feels so self-sufficient
  that he does not need God much.
So he vainly goes on struggling
  to find some explanation
For these disturbing, lonely moods
  of inner isolation.
But the answer keeps eluding him
  for in his selfish, finite mind,
He does not even recognize
  that he cannot ever find
The reason for life's emptiness
  unless he learns to share
The problems and the burdens
  that surround him everywhere.

But when his eyes are opened
   and he looks with love at others,
He begins to see not strangers
   but understanding brothers.
So open up your hardened hearts
   and let God enter in,
He only wants to help you
   a new life to begin.
For every day's a good day
   to lose yourself in others
And any time a good time
   to see mankind as brothers,
And this can only happen
   when you realize it's true
That everyone needs someone
   and that someone is you!

Walking With God

Who cultivates a garden
   and grows flowers from the sod,
Walks hand in hand with nature
   and very close to God.

My only sketch of Heaven is a large blue sky, and a larger one than the biggest I have seen in June—and in it are my friends—every one of them.

                                         Emily Dickinson

Yesterday . . . Today . . . and Tomorrow!

Yesterday's dead, tomorrow's unborn,
So there's nothing to fear and nothing to mourn,
For all that is past and all that has been
Can never return to be lived once again.
And what lies ahead or the things that will be
Are still in God's hands, so it is not up to me
To live in the future that is God's great unknown,
For the past and the present God claims for His own.
So all I need do is to live for today
And trust God to show me the truth and the way.
For it's only the memory of things that have been
And expecting tomorrow to bring trouble again
That fills my today, which God wants to bless,
With uncertain fears and borrowed distress.
For all I need live for is this one little minute
For life's here and now and eternity's in it.

The better part of one's life consists of his friendships.
Abraham Lincoln

Forget-Me-Nots

When to the flowers so beautiful the Father gave a name,
Back came a little blue-eyed one (All timidly it came);
And standing at its Father's feet and gazing in His face,
It said, in low and trembling tone and with a modest grace,
"Dear God, the name Thou gavest me, Alas I have forgot!"
Kindly the Father looked him down and said: "Forget-me-not."

Emily Bruce Roelofson

The bright blue Forget-me-not has been named the state flower of Alaska. The origin of its name supposedly stems from the story of two lovers who were walking by a river when the young lady observed and expressed a desire for a pretty blue flower growing on the river bank. In an effort to please the young lady, the gentleman climbed down the bank and picked some of the blossoms. As he maneuvered, he slipped, fell into the river, and threw the blue flowers onto the bank. As he was swept away by the current, he shouted to his love, "Forget me not."

Thus developed the belief that anyone who wore or carried this flower would experience true love and never be forsaken or forgotten by his or her lover.

Across the Years

Across the years we've met in dreams
And shared each other's hopes and schemes,
We knew a friendship rich and rare
And beauty far beyond compare.
Then you reached out your arms for more,
To catch what you were yearning for.
But little did you think or guess
That one can't capture happiness
Because it's unrestrained and free,
Unfettered by reality.

Years and years of happiness only make us realize how lucky we are to have friends that have shared and made that happiness a reality.
Robert E. Frederick

A Time of Many Miracles

Flowers sleeping 'neath the snow,
Awakening when the spring winds blow;
Leafless trees so bare before,
Gowned in lacy green once more;
Hard, unyielding, frozen sod
Now softly carpeted by God;
Still streams melting in the spring,
Rippling over rocks that sing;
Barren, windswept, lonely hills
Turning gold with daffodils—
These miracles are all around
Within our sight and touch and sound,
As true and wonderful today
As when the stone was rolled away,
Proclaiming to all doubting men
That in God all things live again.

What sunshine is to flowers, smiles are to humanity.
Joseph Addison

My God Is No Stranger

God is no stranger in a faraway place,
He's as close as the wind that blows 'cross my face.
It's true I can't see the wind as it blows
But I feel it around me and my heart surely knows
That God's mighty hand can be felt every minute
For there is nothing on earth that God isn't in it—
The sky and the stars, the waves and the sea,
The dew on the grass, the leaves on a tree
Are constant reminders of God and His nearness,
Proclaiming His presence with crystal-like clearness.
So how could I think God was far, far away
When I feel Him beside me every hour of the day?
And I've plenty of reasons to know God's my Friend
And this is one friendship that time cannot end!

To be capable of steady friendship and lasting love are the two greatest proofs, not only of goodness of heart, but of strength of mind.

William Hazlitt

A Thankful Heart

Take nothing for granted for whenever you do
The joy of enjoying is lessened for you.
For we rob our own lives much more than we know
When we fail to respond or in any way show
Our thanks for the blessings that daily are ours—
The warmth of the sun, the fragrance of flowers,
The beauty of twilight, the freshness of dawn,
The coolness of dew on a green velvet lawn,
The kind little deeds so thoughtfully done,
The favors of friends and the love that someone
Unselfishly gives us in a myriad of ways,
Expecting no payment and no words of praise.
Oh, great is our loss when we no longer find
A thankful response to things of this kind,
For the joy of enjoying and the fullness of living
Are found in the heart that is filled with thanksgiving.

It is a good thing to be rich. It is a good thing to be strong, but it is a better thing to be loved by many friends.

Euripides

Geraniums

The wild geranium holds its dew
Long in the boulder's shade.
William Vaughn Moody

Whenever and wherever herbs are grown or discussed, scented Geraniums are always included. They are unsurpassed for color, fragrance, form, and variety. The Geranium is believed to have been brought from South Africa to England in the seventeenth century. Appealing aromas are released from the leaves of many of the varieties of the Geranium. The fragrances range from scents of almond, lemon, and nutmeg to rose.

The oak-leaved Geranium has its own peculiar oily-sweet scent. It represents true friendship.

The Geranium's message is one of calm, spiritual happiness and smiles.

My Garden

My garden beautifies my yard
    and adds fragrance to the air,
But it is also my cathedral
   and my quiet place of prayer.
So little do we realize
   that the glory and the power
Of He who made the universe
   lies hidden in a flower.

A man who could make one rose would be accounted most won-
derful yet God scatters countless such flowers around us.

                                                    Martin Luther

Everyone Needs Someone

People need people and friends need friends,
And we all need love for a full life depends
Not on vast riches or great acclaim,
Not on success or on worldly fame
But just in knowing that someone cares
And holds us close in thoughts and prayers.
For only the knowledge that we're understood
Makes everyday living feel wonderfully good.
And we rob ourselves of life's greatest need
When we lock up our hearts and fail to heed
The outstretched hand reaching to find
A kindred spirit whose heart and mind
Are lonely and longing to somehow share
Our joys and sorrows and to make us aware
That life's completeness and richness depends
On the things we share with loved ones and friends.

*So long as we love, we serve. So long as we are loved by others,
I would say we were indispensable; and no person is useless while
he or she has a friend.*

Robert Louis Stevenson

I Think of You And
I Pray for You, Too

Often during a busy day
I pause for a minute
    to silently pray.
I mention the names
    of those I love
And treasured friends
    I am fondest of.
For it doesn't matter
    where we pray
If we honestly mean
    the words that we say,
For God is always
    listening to hear
The prayers that are made
    by a heart that's sincere.

My friend is not perfect no more than I am, and so we suit each other admirably.

Alexander Pope

The Gift of Friendship

Friendship is a priceless gift
   that cannot be bought or sold,
But its value is far greater
   than a mountain made of gold.
For gold is cold and lifeless,
   it can neither see nor hear,
And in the time of trouble
   it is powerless to cheer.
It has no ears to listen
   no heart to understand,
It cannot bring you comfort
   or reach out a helping hand.
So when you ask God for a gift,
   be thankful if He sends
Not diamonds, pearls, or riches,
   but the love of real true friends.

Make new friends, but keep the old, one is silver and the other is gold.

Joseph Parry

The Answer

In the beauty
  of a snowflake
    falling softly on the land,

Is the mystery
  and the miracle
    of God's great, creative hand.

In the tiny petal
  of a tiny flower
    that grew from a tiny pod,

Is the miracle
  and the mystery
    of all creation and God!

A friend should be loved freely for himself, and not for anything else.
Saint Augustine

Strangers Are Friends
We Haven't Met

God knows no strangers,
He loves us all,
The poor, the rich,
The great, the small.
He is a Friend
Who is always there
To share our troubles
And lessen our care.
No one is a stranger
In God's sight,
For God is love
And in His light
May we, too, try
In our small way
To make new friends
From day to day.
So pass no stranger
With an unseeing eye,
For God may be sending
A new friend by.

There is no possession more valuable than a good and faithful friend.
Socrates

Hyacinths

And the Hyacinth . . . purple, white, and blue,
Which flung from its bells a sweet peal anew
Of music so delicate, soft, and intense,
It was felt like an odour within the sense.

Percy Bysshe Shelley

Bowls of Hyacinths add color, fragrance, and welcome to any home. It is said that Madame de Pompadour increased the popularity of Hyacinths when she started placing arrangements of them in the palace and ordered her gardeners to cultivate the bulbs indoors during the winter months so that she could enjoy the fragrance all year.

In the language of flowers, Hyacinths stand for sport, games, and fair play.

Friends Are Really Wonderful
But Special Ones Are Few

Friends are really wonderful,
   but special ones are few
And they simply don't make them
   more special than you.
For who but a wonderful friend
   would be
As thoughtful and nice
   as you've been to me?
And you'll never know
   how many times through the year
I sing your praises
   for the world to hear.
It's no wonder I welcome
   an occasion like this
To send you best wishes
   and a big hello kiss.
So consider yourself
   most exuberantly kissed,
For you're one of the specials
   on my friendship list.

A true friend knows when you need a word of affection and encouragement, and knows just how to say it.

Norman Vincent Peale

All Nature Tells Us
Nothing Really Ever Dies

Nothing really ever dies
That is not born anew,
The miracles of nature
All tell us this is true.
The flowers sleeping peacefully
Beneath the winter's snow
Awaken from their icy grave
When spring winds start to blow.
And little brooks and singing streams,
Icebound beneath the snow,
Begin to babble merrily
Beneath the sun's warm glow.
And all around on every side
New life and joy appear
To tell us nothing ever dies
And we should have no fear,
For death is just a detour
Along life's wending way
That leads God's chosen children
To a bright and glorious day.

Things do not change, we do.
Henry David Thoreau

God Knows Best

Our Father knows what's best for us,
So why should we complain;
We always want the sunshine,
But He knows there must be rain.
We love the sound of laughter
And the merriment of cheer,
But our hearts would lose their tenderness
If we never shed a tear.
Our Father tests us often
With suffering and with sorrow,
He tests us, not to punish us,
But to help us meet tomorrow.
For growing trees are strengthened
When they withstand the storm,
And the sharp cut of the chisel
Gives the marble grace and form.
God never hurts us needlessly,
And He never wastes our pain,
For every loss He sends to us
Is followed by rich gain.
And when we count the blessings
That God has so freely sent,
We will find no cause for murmuring
And no time to lament.

For our Father loves His children,
And to Him all things are plain,
So He never sends us pleasure
When the soul's deep need is pain.
So whenever we are troubled,
And when everything goes wrong,
It is just God working in us
To make our spirits strong.
And every individual,
As well as every nation,
Will find that in adversity
There is always compensation.
For men as well as nations
Must take lessons in the school
That teaches by experience
That the plain old Golden Rule
Is still the best to live by,
For its sheer simplicity
Insures a peaceful universe
Where every man is free.

Thank You, God, for Everything

Thank You, God, for everything,
    the big things and the small,
For every good gift comes from God
    the Giver of them all.
And all too often we accept
    without any thanks or praise
The gifts God sends as blessings
    each day in many ways.
And so at this time
    we offer up a prayer
To thank You, God, for giving us
    a lot more than our share . . .
First, thank You for the little things
    that often come our way,
The things we take for granted
    but don't mention when we pray,
Then, thank You for the miracles
    we are much too blind to see,
And give us new awareness
    of our many gifts from Thee,
And help us to remember
    that the key to life and living
Is to make each prayer a prayer of thanks
    and every day Thanksgiving.

To be rich in friends is to be poor in nothing.
Lillian Whiting

One of the Author's Favorite Prayers

God, open my eyes so I may see
And feel Your presence close to me.
Give me strength for my stumbling feet
As I battle the crowd on life's busy street,
And widen the vision of my unseeing eyes,
So in passing faces I'll recognize
Not just a stranger, unloved and unknown,
But a friend with a heart that is much like my own.
Give me perception to make me aware
That scattered profusely on life's thoroughfare
Are the best gifts of God that we daily pass by
As we look at the world with an unseeing eye.

He who sows courtesy reaps friendship, and he who plants kindness
gathers love.

Author Unknown

Laurel

Pile laurel wreaths upon his grave
Who did not gain, but was, success.
Joyce Kilmer

Laurel is an evergreen tree that can attain a height of forty feet but usually reaches only four to ten feet. A native of the Mediterranean region, it is widely cultivated for its elegant appearance and the pleasant aromatic fragrance of its evergreen leaves. The glossy leaves are known to cooks as bay leaves and afford a distinctive flavor frequently called for in recipes.

Laurel was used in the victory wreaths in classical Greek and Roman times and bestowed as a distinction of honor on poets and heroes. The phrase *Poet Laureate* is derived from this age-old practice.

I Count My Blessings

When I count my blessings
    I count my fans as one,
For without fans and friends
    the writing I have done
Would lose all its meaning,
    its warmth, and sincereness,
For how could I write
    without feeling a nearness
To all the dear people
    who interpret each line
With their own love and kindness
    which becomes part of mine?
So more than you know
    I thank God up above
For fans, friends, and family
    and their gifts of love.

Friendship is always a sweet responsibility, never an opportunity.
                                    Kahlil Gibran

Finding Faith in a Flower

Sometimes when faith is running low
And I cannot fathom why things are so,
I walk alone among the flowers I grow
And learn the answers to all I would know.
For among my flowers I have come to see
Life's miracle and its mystery.
And standing in silence and reverie
My faith comes flooding back to me!

The miracles of nature do not seem miracles because they are so
common. If no one had ever seen a flower, even a dandelion would
be the most startling event in the world.

Author Unknown

The Praying Hands

The Praying Hands are much, much more
   than just a work of art,
They are the soul's creation
   of a deeply thankful heart.
They are a priceless masterpiece
   that love alone could paint,
And they reveal the selflessness
   of an unheralded saint.
These hands so scarred and toilworn
   tell the story of a man
Who sacrificed his talent
   in accordance with God's plan.
For in God's plan are many things
   man cannot understand,
But we must trust God's judgment
   and be guided by His hand.
Sometimes He asks us to give up
   our dreams of happiness,
Sometimes we must forgo our hopes
   of fortune and success.
Not all of us can triumph
   or rise to heights of fame,
And many times what should be ours
   goes to another name.

But he who makes a sacrifice
   so another may succeed
Is indeed a true disciple
   of our blessed Savior's creed.
For when we give ourselves away
   in sacrifice and love,
We are laying up rich treasures
   in God's kingdom up above.
And hidden in gnarled, toilworn hands
   is the truest art of living,
Achieved alone by those who've learned
   the victory of giving.
For any sacrifice on earth
   made in the dear Lord's name
Assures the giver of a place
   in heaven's Hall of Fame.
And who can say with certainty
Where the greatest talent lies,
Or who will be the greatest
In our heavenly Father's eyes?
And who can tell with certainty
   in the heavenly Father's sight
Who's entitled to the medals
   and who's the hero of the fight?

Following in His Footsteps

When someone does a kindness
 it always seems to me
That's the way God up in heaven
 would like us all to be.
For when we bring some pleasure
 to another human heart
We have followed in His footsteps
 and we've had a little part
In serving Him who loves us . . .
 for I am very sure it's true
That in serving those around us
 we serve and please Him, too.

The best way to cheer yourself up is to try to cheer up somebody else.

Mark Twain

After the Winter, God Sends the Spring

Springtime is a season
Of hope and joy and cheer.
There's beauty all around us
To see and touch and hear.
So, no matter how downhearted
And discouraged we may be,
New hope is born when we behold
Leaves budding on a tree.
Or when we see a timid flower
Push through the frozen sod
And open wide in glad surprise
Its petaled eyes to God.
For this is just God saying,
"Lift up your eyes to Me,
And the bleakness of your spirit,
Like the budding springtime tree,
Will lose its wintry darkness
And your heavy heart will sing."
For God never sends the winter
Without the joy of spring.

If spring came but once in a century instead of once a year, or burst forth with the sound of an earthquake and not in silence, what wonder and expectation there would be in all hearts to behold the miraculous change.

Henry Wadsworth Longfellow

Lilies

And why do you worry about clothes?
See how the lilies of the field grow.
They do not labor or spin.
Yet, I tell you that
not even Solomon in all his splendor
was dressed like one of these.
                              Matthew 6:28

The white Lily is an emblem of majesty and purity. It is thought to have been in existence since well before the Ice Age, and has survived the test of time.

Legends associated with the Lily have religious connotations. For centuries, artists painted white Lilies in the hands of the angel Gabriel when he came to Mary to announce that it was she who would become the mother of the Christ Child, Jesus.

The Lily is also the sign of the Resurrection, and as such is closely associated with Easter and is designated as the Easter flower. Altars are banked with Lilies of all sizes during Easter services and lend their own touch of inspiration, solemnity, and symbolism.

Known as the flower of beauty, the Madonna Lily was transported to England by the Romans solely for the therapeutic qualities of its juices. The application of those juices was believed to relieve the pain and discomfort of the tired and aching feet of the soldiers following long marches, as well as to heal corns and calluses on the feet.

In God's Tomorrow
There Is Eternal Spring

All nature heeds the call of spring
As God awakens everything,
And all that seemed so dead and still
Experiences a sudden thrill
As springtime lays a magic hand
Across God's vast and fertile land.
Oh, how can anyone stand by
And watch a sapphire springtime sky
Or see a fragile flower break through
What just a day ago or two
Seemed barren ground still hard with frost.
But in God's world no life is lost,
And flowers sleep beneath the ground,
But when they hear spring's waking sound
They push themselves through layers of clay
To reach the sunlight of God's day.
And man, like flowers, too, must sleep
Until he is called from the darkened deep
To live in that place where angels sing
And where there is eternal spring!

Life without friendship is like the sky without the sun.
Author Unknown

Life's Gift of Love

If people like me
   didn't know people like you,
Life would lose its meaning
   and its richness, too.
For the friends that we make
   are life's gift of love,
And I think friends are sent
   right from heaven above.
And thinking of you
   somehow makes me feel
That God is love
   and He's very real.

A real friend is one who walks in when the rest of the world walks out.

Walter Winchell

The Legend of the Raindrop

The legend of the raindrop
Has a lesson for us all
As it trembled in the heavens
Questioning whether it should fall.
For the glistening raindrop argued
To the genie of the sky,
"I am beautiful and lovely
As I sparkle here on high,
And hanging here I will become
Part of the rainbow's hue
And I'll shimmer like a diamond
For all the world to view."
But the genie told the raindrop,
"Do not hesitate to go,
For you will be more beautiful
If you fall to earth below.

For you will sink into the soil
And be lost awhile from sight,
But when you reappear on earth,
You'll be looked on with delight.
For you will be the raindrop
That quenched the thirsty ground
And helped the lovely flowers
To blossom all around,
And in your resurrection
You'll appear in queenly clothes
With the beauty of the lily
And the fragrance of the rose;
Then, when you wilt and wither,
You'll become part of the earth
And make the soil more fertile
And give new flowers birth'' . . .
For there is nothing ever lost
Or eternally neglected,
For everything God ever made
Is always resurrected.

Light a Candle

An unlit candle gives no light,
Only when it's burning, is it shining bright.
And life is empty, dull, and dark,
Until doing things for others gives the needed spark
That sets a useless life on fire
And fills the heart with new desire.

The light of friendship is like the light of phosphorous—seen plainest when all around is dark.

William Crowell

The Golden Chain of Friendship

Friendship is a golden chain,
The links are friends so dear,
And like a rare and precious jewel
It's treasured more each year.
It's clasped together firmly
With a love that's deep and true,
And it's rich with happy memories
And fond recollections, too.
Time can't destroy its beauty
For, as long as memory lives,
Years can't erase the pleasure
That the joy of friendship gives.
For the golden chain of friendship
Is a strong and blessed tie
Binding kindred hearts together
As the years go passing by.

Friendship cheers like a sunbeam; charms like a good story; inspires like a brave leader; binds like a golden chain; guides like a heavenly vision.

Newell Dwight Hillis

Pansies

There is Pansies, that's for thoughts.
William Shakespeare

The name for the wild Pansy came from the French word *pensée,* meaning "thought." It is rumored that during the days of King Arthur and his knights if a Pansy was found with seven streaks on its petals, it indicated constancy in love, but eight streaks predicted fickleness. Of course, the knights sought the Pansies with seven streaks on the petals.

Names that have been given to the Pansy through the years include "Kiss Me at the Garden Gate," "Lovers' Thoughts," "Heartease," and "Eyebright."

The Peace of Meditation

So we may know God better
    and feel His quiet power
Let us all begin the day
    with a meditation hour.
For our Father tells His children
    that if they would know His will
They must seek Him in the silence
    when all is calm and still.
For nature's greatest forces
    are found in quiet things
Like softly falling snowflakes
    drifting down on angels' wings,
Or petals dropping soundlessly
    from a lovely full-blown rose,
So God comes closest to us
    when our souls are in repose.
For when everything is quiet
    and when we're lost in meditation,
Our soul is then preparing
    for a deeper dedication
That will make it wholly possible
    to quietly endure
The violent world around us
    for in God we are secure.

The only rose without thorns is friendship.
Magdeleine de Scudéry

Spring Awakens
What Autumn Puts to Sleep

A garden of asters of varying hues,
Crimson pinks and violet blues,
Blossoming in the hazy fall
Wrapped in autumn's lazy pall.
But early frost stole in one night
And like a chilling, killing blight
It touched each pretty aster's head
And now the garden's still and dead.
And all the lovely flowers that bloomed
Will soon be buried and entombed
In winter's icy shroud of snow.
But, oh, how wonderful to know
That after winter comes the spring
To breathe new life into everything.
And all the flowers that fell in death
Will be awakened by spring's breath.
For in God's plan both men and flowers
Can only reach bright, shining hours
By dying first to rise in glory
And prove again the great, great story.

Deep in their roots all flowers keep the light.
Theodore Roethke

A Friend Is a Gift of God

Among the great and glorious gifts
    our heavenly Father sends
Is the gift of understanding
    that we find in loving friends.
For, somehow, in the generous heart
    of loving, faithful friends
The good God in His charity
    and wisdom always sends
A sense of understanding
    and the power of perception
And mixes these fine qualities
    with kindness and affection.
So when we need some sympathy
    or a friendly hand to touch,
Or an ear that listens tenderly
    and speaks words that mean so much,
We seek our true and trusted friend
    in the knowledge that we'll find
A heart that's sympathetic
    and an understanding mind.
And often just without a word
    there seems to be a union
Of thoughts and kindred feelings
    for God gives true friends communion.

Friendships are the fruits gathered from the trees planted in the rich soil of love, and nurtured with tender care and understanding.

Alma L. Weixelbaum

I'm Glad That We Met

I'm glad our paths crossed
   and I'm glad that we met,
And may this brief interlude
   prove to be, yet,
Something that helped
   to open the door
To the niche in life
   you were destined for.
For all that transpires,
   be it bitter or sweet,
Helps to make your life's pattern
   a bit more complete.
And sometime in the future
   may you look back and say
Our meeting was indeed a
   very lucky day.

Go often to the house of a friend, for weeds choke the unused path.
Ralph Waldo Emerson

On Life's Busy Thoroughfares
We Meet With Angels Unaware

The unexpected kindness
   from an unexpected place,
A hand outstretched in friendship,
   a smile on someone's face,
A word of understanding
   spoken in an hour of trial
Are unexpected miracles
   that make life more worthwhile.
We know not how it happened
   that in an hour of need
Somebody out of nowhere
   proved to be a friend indeed.
For God has many messengers
   we fail to recognize,
But He sends them when we need them
   for His ways are wondrous wise!
So keep looking for an angel
   and keep listening to hear,
For on life's busy crowded streets
   you will find God's presence near.

*Friendship that flows from the heart cannot be frozen by adversity,
as the water that flows from the spring cannot congeal in winter.*
James Fenimore Cooper

Who Do You Work For?

I work for God
And I work for His glory
In all that I do
I retell the old story—
The story of life
And how we should live
And how we should share
And continuously give.

When sowing seeds of friendly deeds, the less you keep, the more you reap.

Christopher Bannister

Roses

Here is proof of a Creator: God made manifest;
In this little rose we see divinity expressed.

                                        Patience Strong

The Rose is called the queen of flowers and has been growing
for millions of years. It is thought to be the first flower cultivated
by man. There are many varieties of Roses, each with a story of
its own. The Resurrection flower, also known as the Rose of
Jericho, is believed to have first bloomed at the Birth of Christ,
to have closed its blooms at the time of the Crucifixion, only to
reopen at the time of the Resurrection. The folklore of the Rose
also includes the fact that the five petals of the white Rose rep-
resent the five wounds of Jesus Christ.

The Rose is the emblem of beauty. The white Rose has been
associated with silence, sworn friendship, and a promise not to
reveal secrets. The expression *Sub Rosa* stems from the custom
of having a white Rose present to guarantee that transpiring con-
versations would not be repeated. For many years, starting with
the Romans up to Victorian days, a Rose adorned wine and
toasting cups, embellished plastered ceilings in dining rooms,
and was carved over the door of confessionals in European ca-
thedrals.

Roses Always Make a
Garden a Bit More Lovely

Like roses in a garden,
   kindness fills the air
With a certain bit of sweetness
   as it touches everywhere.
For kindness is a circle
   that never, never ends
But just keeps ever-widening
   in the circle of our friends.
For happiness is only found
   in bringing it to others
And thinking of the folks next door
   as sisters and as brothers.
For the more you give, the more you get
   is proven every day,
And so to get the most from life
   you must give yourself away.
And if this greedy world today
   would only start to give
Life everywhere for everyone
   would be more sweet to live.

If we really want to love, we must first learn how to forgive.
Mother Teresa

My Dear Friend

You're like a ray of sunshine
Or a star up in the sky,
You add a special brightness
Whenever you pass by.
And all your lovely thoughts, dear,
That make my heart rejoice
Are spoken very clearly
By your loving heart's still voice.
For in this raucous, restless world
We're small but God is great,
And in His love, dear friend,
Our hearts communicate!

A friend is long sought, hardly found, and with difficulty, kept.
Saint Jerome

Life's Fairest Flower

I have a garden within my soul
Of wondrous beauty rare,
Wherein the blossoms of my life
Bloom ever in splendor fair.

The fragrance and charm of that garden,
Where all of life's flowers bloom,
Fills my aching heart with sweet content
And banishes failure's gloom.

Each flower a message is bringing,
A memory of someone dear,
A picture of deepest devotion,
Dispelling all doubt and fear.

Amid all this beauty and splendor,
One flower stands forth as queen,
Alone in her dazzling beauty,
Alone but ever supreme.

This flower of love and devotion
Has guided me all through life,
Softening my grief and my sorrow,
Sharing my toil and my strife.

This flower has helped me to conquer
Temptation so black and grim
And led me to victory and honor
Over my enemy, sin.

I have vainly sought in my garden,
Through blossoms of love and light,
For a flower of equal wonder
To compare with this one so bright.

But ever I've met with failure,
My search has been in vain,
For never a flower existed,
Like the blossom I can claim.

For after years I now can see,
Amid life's roses and rue,
God's greatest gift to a little child,
My darling mother, was you.

Flowers Leave Their Fragrance
On the Hand That Bestows Them

This old Chinese proverb,
  if practiced each day,
Would change the whole world
  in a wonderful way.
Its truth is so simple,
  it's so easy to do,
And it works every time
  and successfully, too.
For you can't do a kindness
  without a reward,
Not in silver nor gold
  but in joy from the Lord.
You can't light a candle
  to show others the way
Without feeling the warmth
  of the bright little ray.
And you can't pluck a rose,
  all fragrant with dew,
Without part of its fragrance
  remaining with you.

Those who bring sunshine into the lives of others cannot keep it from themselves.

James Matthew Barrie

I've Never Seen God

I've never seen God
   but I know how I feel,
It's people like you
   who make Him so real.
God doesn't ask me
   to weep when I pray,
It seems that I pass Him
   so often each day
In the faces of people
   I meet on my way.
He's the stars in the heaven,
   a smile on some face,
A leaf on a tree,
   or a rose in a vase.
He's winter and autumn
   and summer and spring,
In short, God is every
   real and wonderful thing.
I wish I might meet Him
   much more than I do,
I would if there were
   more people like you.

Friendship without self-interest is one of the rare and beautiful things of life.

James Francis Byrnes

Snowdrops and Crocuses

Crocus . . . "it maketh the English sprightly."
Francis Bacon

Snowdrops and Crocuses are always a welcomed sight. They are the very first harbingers of early spring. Often they pop up in a layer of snow to tell of better days to come and to bid good-bye to winter. Their message is one of hope and of promise.

The Flower of Friendship

Life is like a garden
And friendship like a flower
That blooms and grows in beauty
With the sunshine and the shower.

And lovely are the blossoms
That are tended with great care
By those who work unselfishly
To make the place more fair.

And in the garden of the heart
Friendship's flower opens wide
When we shower it with kindness
As our love shines from inside.

The true friend seeks to give, not to take; to help, not to be helped; to minister, not to be ministered unto.

William Rader

Give Lavishly! Live Abundantly!

The more you give,
  the more you get.
The more you laugh,
  the less you fret.
The more you do
  unselfishly,
The more you live
  abundantly.
The more of everything
  you share,
The more you'll always
  have to spare.
The more you love,
  the more you'll find
That life is good
  and friends are kind.
For only what
  we give away,
Enriches us
  from day to day.

Friendship improves happiness and abates misery by doubling our joy and dividing our grief.

Joseph Addison

Friendship's Touch

I seldom see you through the year,
We've met so very rarely, dear.
We've never talked together much
And yet we've both felt friendship's touch.
So many things we can't explain,
The sun . . . the stars . . . the wind . . . the rain . . .
And yet we know that Someone above
Holds all the answers in His love.
I got your lovely little note
And in between the lines you wrote
I felt a hand reach out to mine
And saw a smile like warm sunshine.
Now who can say just what makes a friend
Or why one heart and another blend?
And who can say what secret lies
Behind somebody else's eyes?

I only know that I reach out
And love engulfs me all about,
For God is love and He's everywhere
So there is plenty of love to share.
And all God's children are only a part
Of a universal, eternal heart,
And often the heart finds cause to rejoice
At words that are said by the soul's still voice.
So I'll tell you again as I have before,
Each day I realize more and more
That all that I write and all that I do
Is inspired by people just like you.
So the beauty you find in the lines I write
Are but a reflection of your own inner light.
And I'm thankful and blessed that my words can be sent
To friends who feel what I really meant!

April

April comes with cheeks a-glowing,
Silver streams are all a-flowing,
Flowers open wide their eyes
In a rapturous surprise.
Lilies dream beside the brooks,
Violets in meadow nooks,
And the birds gone wild with glee
Fill the woods with melody.

Winds are soft and fields are fair,
Blue the sky and sweet the air,
And the happy, blushing earth
Laughs at every flower's birth.
Golden days and silver nights,
Hours brim with calm delights,
Lilies chime and bluebells ring,
"Welcome, welcome to the spring."

The Amen! of Nature is always a flower.
Oliver Wendell Holmes

No Hands Are Empty
That Serve Others

What can I do?
I've so little to give,
How can I show
Someone else how to live
When I hardly know how
To manage my day?
But I plead with my heart,
Teach me to pray!

*The only reward of virtue is virtue; the only way to have a friend
is to be one.*

Ralph Waldo Emerson

Tulips

Corridors, like windy tulip beds,
Of swaying girls and lifted, tossing heads.
                                        David Morton

Tulips are not mentioned in ancient literature. It is believed that they were introduced into England during the reign of Elizabeth I, having been brought from Turkey and Vienna. "Tulipmania" erupted in Holland during the years 1625 to 1635, and Tulip bulbs, considered valuable, were extremely costly. The red Tulip suggests a declaration of love, whereas the wild or yellow Tulip is known as a symbol of hopeless love.

Tulips also offer the message to guard your own "two lips" and to use them to speak only kind words to or about others.

Listen in Silence
If You Would Hear

Silently the green leaves grow,
In silence falls the soft, white snow;
Silently the flowers bloom,
In silence sunshine fills a room;
Silently bright stars appear,
In silence velvet night draws near;
And silently God enters in
To free a troubled heart from sin.
For God works silently in lives,
And nothing spiritual survives
Amid the din of a noisy street,
Where raucous crowds with hurrying feet
And blinded eyes and deafened ear
Are never privileged to hear
The message God wants to impart
To every troubled, weary heart.
For only in a quiet place
Can man behold God face-to-face!

Be still, and know that I am God.

*What sweetness is left in life, if you take away friendship? Robbing
life of friendship is like robbing the world of the sun.*

Cicero

Help Us to See and Understand

God, give us wider vision
    to see and understand
That both the sun and showers
    are gifts from Thy great hand.
And when our lives are overcast
    with trouble and with care,
Give us the faith to see beyond
    the dark clouds of despair.
Teach us that it takes the showers
    to make the flowers grow
And only in the storms of life
    when the winds of trouble blow
Can man, too, reach maturity
    and grow in faith and grace
And gain the strength and courage
    to enable him to face
Sunny days as well as rain,
    high peaks as well as low,
Knowing that the April showers
    will make the May flowers grow.
And then at last may we accept
    the sunshine and the showers,
Confident it takes them both
    to make salvation ours!

The best and most beautiful things in the world cannot be seen or even touched. They must be felt with the heart.

Helen Keller

Things to Be Thankful For

The good, green earth beneath our feet,
The air we breathe, the food we eat,
Some work to do, a goal to win,
A hidden longing deep within
That spurs us on to bigger things
And helps us meet what each day brings,
All these things and many more
Are things we should be thankful for.

And something else we should not forget—
That people we've known or heard of or met
By indirection have had a big part
In molding the thoughts of the mind and the heart.
And so it's the people who are like you
That people like me should give thanks to,
For no one can live to himself alone
And no one can win just on his own.
Too bad there aren't a whole lot more
People like you to be thankful for.

I am a part of all that I have met.
Alfred, Lord Tennyson

It's a Wonderful World

It's a wonderful world
   and it's people like you
Who make it that way
   by the things that they do.
For a warm, ready smile,
   or a kind, thoughtful deed,
Or a hand outstretched
   in an hour of need
Can change our whole outlook
   and make the world bright
Where a minute before
   just nothing seemed right.
It's a wonderful world
   and it always will be
If we keep our eyes open
   and focused to see
The wonderful things
   man is capable of
When he opens his heart
   to God and His love.

No life is so strong and complete, but that it yearns for the smile of a friend.

Wallace Bruce

Violets

Blue! Gentle cousin of the forest-green,
Married to green in all the sweetest flowers—
Forget-me-not,—the blue bell,—
and that Queen
Of secrecy, the violet.

John Keats

Remember as a child romping through the woods and stopping long enough to gather a bouquet of purple Violets? The history of the Violet dates back to ancient Greece, where Violets were cultivated for their fragrance. Through the years, Violets have been used in homes and palaces to overcome musty and damp odors. In early days, a wreath or garland of Violets was worn in the hair at weddings. Through the years, Violets have been nibbled as tasty treats and, more recently, dipped in melted chocolate as a gourmet sweet or decoration.

Violets stand for modesty.

Everywhere Across the Land You See God's Face and Touch His Hand

Each time you look up in the sky
Or watch the fluffy clouds drift by,
Or feel the sunshine warm and bright,
Or watch the dark night turn to light,
Or hear a bluebird sweetly sing,
Or see the winter turn to spring,
Or stop to pick a daffodil,
Or gather violets on some hill,
Or touch a leaf or see a tree,
It's all God whispering, "This is Me . . .
And I am faith and I am light
And in Me there shall be no night."

Friendship is the nearest thing we know to religion. God is love, and to make religion akin to friendship is simply to give it the expression conceivable by man.

John Ruskin

Not by Chance Nor Happenstance

Into our lives come many things
   to break the dull routine,
The things we had not planned on
   that happen unforeseen,
The unexpected little joys
   that are scattered on our way,
Success we did not count on
   or a rare, fulfilling day,
An unsought word of kindness,
   a compliment or two
That set the eyes to gleaming
   like crystal drops of dew,
The unplanned sudden meeting
   that comes with sweet surprise
And lights the heart with happiness
   like a rainbow in the skies.
Now some folks call it fickle fate
   and some folks call it chance,
While others just accept it
   as a pleasant happenstance.
But no matter what you call it,
   it didn't come without design,
For all our lives are fashioned
   by the hand that is Divine.

We secure our friends not by accepting favors but by doing them.
                                   Thucydides

My Thanks

I owe thanks to many people
    for all they've done for me,
And my heart is just as grateful
    as a human heart can be.
But a mortal heart is much too small
    to fully comprehend
The magnitude of thankfulness
    that is due a trusted friend,
And while I mean sincerely
    every word and line and phrase
That I utter at this season
    filled with thankfulness and praise,
I somehow feel inadequate
    to find words that will describe
The intensity of the gratitude
    I feel so deep inside.
For little words and phrases
    seem less than nothingness
To describe the thoughts of thankfulness
    I am longing to express.
And I cannot help but wonder
    if these futile words of mine
Are another indication,
    an evidence and sign
That nothing mortal man can say
    is ever quite complete,
For even in our victory
    we are conscious of defeat.

And again I am defeated
    as I am each time I try
To express my deep emotions
    and explain the unknown why.
For true communication
    is reached through God alone
For by Him the thoughts we can't express
    are understood and known.
And He transmits the message
    our words cannot formulate,
And so at this present time
    may the Lord communicate
The loving thanks and gratitude
    I'm unable to express
And may He visit you today
    and may His presence bless
Your home and heart with thankfulness
    and lasting happiness.
And may the many, many things
    that I cannot say
Become a living truth to you
    as you lift your hands to pray.

Thank You for Your Friendship

Thank you for your friendship
And your understanding of
The folks who truly love you
And the folks you truly love.

A poet once these words penned, a man is rich who has a friend . . .
I read it and thought how true, he must have had a friend like you.

Author Unknown

The World Needs Friendly Folks Like You

In this troubled world
   it's refreshing to find
Someone who still has
   the time to be kind,
Someone who still has
   the faith to believe
That the more you give
   the more you receive,
Someone who's ready
   by thought, word, or deed
To reach out a hand,
   in the hour of need.

The only true gift is a portion of thyself.
Ralph Waldo Emerson

Now this book has ended
You've read the pages through
How grateful must be your friend
To have a friend like you!

For this gift from the giver was given
Wrapped with love and kindness and thought
In heartfelt appreciation
For the joy that your friendship has brought.

VJR